FROM UNNOTICED TO BEING REMEMBERED

A ROADMAP TO GET MAGNETIC PERSONALITY

FARHA KHAN

Made with ♥ on the Notion Press Platform
www.notionpress.com

This work is dedicated to my parents for instilling in me the habit of jotting down everything in one place. Their constant support and encouragement made this book possible.

Contents

Foreword

This book delves into personality enhancement techniques, covering all the intricate details necessary to cultivate a robust personality. Because nothing goes unnoticed, every aspect counts,from your appearance and attire to your overall vibe. The mindset you uphold serves as the cornerstone of your personality, encompassing morals and high values that distinguish you as a branded individual.

Infusing aesthetics into your mundane lifestyle can illuminate your personality. You can initiate lifestyle changes by incorporating small habits and shedding others. The sense of stagnation you experience when things don't seem to align can be transformed through mindset shifts, as outlined in the chapter on paradigm change.

When you begin to embrace honesty with yourself, your vibe becomes irresistibly magnetic. People not only take notice of you but also remember you long after you have left the room. Your vibe precedes you even before you utter a word in a crowded space. While not everyone may appreciate you, a strong magnetic personality inevitably attracts envious eyes. Rather than seeking universal approval, strive to be remembered by all.

The ultimate objective is to imprint our thoughts and personality onto others, leaving an indelible mark. Be unforgettable, and your spark will be impossible to extinguish. So,welcome aboard the journey to becoming an irresistible and magnetic individual.

Preface

The content of this book is akin to that of my dear diary. It chronicles a journey of self-growth; once I meticulously documented everything in my journal, and now it encapsulates the transition from journaling to authorship, from addressing "dear diary" to addressing "dear reader." It serves as a roadmap to personal transformation.

This book serves as a foundational guide to enhancing your personality. As someone prone to overthinking, I stumbled upon various tricks and tips that I have inadvertently adopted. I have avidly read books and prided myself on being a diligent researcher, well, at least that's what I believe about myself, (smiley face). I have maintained a journal since childhood, jotting down grooming tips, and indulging in what some might consider typical "girl stuff" like makeup and fashion.

I am quite talkative, and many of the insights shared in this book stem from casual conversations with diverse individuals. Encouraged by my parents, I have compiled these insights into a book format, hoping they might be beneficial to readers. After much contemplation, this marks my inaugural venture into the world of publishing. Ta-da!

Acknowledgements

I am profoundly grateful to Almighty God for making this happen. I want to express my deepest love for my parents, for their unconditional love and support. The content of this book is the fruit of their teachings and the lessons they imparted to me during difficult times.I also want to thank my brothers for their motivation and love, as well as my soul friends for their steadfast presence.

I wish to express my sincere gratitude to Prof. Achint Chugh, my esteemed boss, for his invaluable support in both my professional growth and personal development. Working alongside you has been a delight. The truest gentleman I have ever had the honour to encounter. Furthermore, I am deeply appreciative of Dr. Arpan Dwivedi, renowned author of technical literature such as" Embedded Systems with Arduino and Its Applications", whose guidance and encouragement have been instrumental in realizing this personal project. Your encouragement has enabled me to check off an item on my bucket list.I am profoundly indebted to you for your unwavering support during my most challenging moments.

Prologue

This book delves into personality enhancement techniques, covering all the intricate details necessary to cultivate a robust personality. Because nothing goes unnoticed, every aspect counts,from your appearance and attire to your overall vibe. The mindset you uphold serves as the cornerstone of your personality, encompassing morals and high values that distinguish you as a branded individual.

Infusing aesthetics into your mundane lifestyle can illuminate your personality. You can initiate lifestyle changes by incorporating small habits and shedding others. The sense of stagnation you experience when things don't seem to align seem to align can be transformed through mindset shifts, as outlined in the chapter on paradigm change.

When you begin to embrace honesty with yourself, your vibe becomes irresistibly magnetic. People not only take notice of you but also remember you long after you have left the room. Your vibe precedes you even before you utter a word in a crowded space. While not everyone may appreciate you, a strong magnetic personality inevitably attracts envious eyes. Rather than seeking universal approval, strive to be remembered by all.

The ultimate objective is to imprint our thoughts and personality onto others, leaving an indelible mark. Be unforgettable, and your spark will be impossible to extinguish. So, welcome aboard the journey to becoming an irresistible and magnetic individual.

CHAPTER ONE

HOW TO ALWAYS LOOK PUT TOGETHER?

As we've all heard, **"First impression is the last impression."** To be memorable, one should maintain a clean and polished appearance. An elegant person does not seek attention but rather exudes effortless attractiveness. Therefore, to achieve a polished look, one must aim for statement looks, ensuring they are well put together and elegant for any occasion.

As Coco Chanel famously said, **"A girl should be two things; classy and fabulous."** Chanel, the renowned French designer, is celebrated for her classy innovations. This chapter provides comprehensive details on how to effortlessly achieve beauty and class.

Grace, respect, class, and elegance are qualities that define a true lady. To embody these traits, one should cultivate proper etiquette and refined manners to achieve a more poised demeanour.While there are no strict rules for being a lady, maintaining a polished physical appearance along with mental stability is essential. Additionally, learning time management and financial management skills will help you stand out from the crowd.Furthermore, strive to be a person of generosity and kindness.

"Fashion fades, only style remains the same ",Coco Chanel.

- **GET A SIGNATURE LOOK:**

To stand out from the crowd, one must possess a particular fashion sense. It is not necessary to be ultra-rich or a fashionista to look stunningly gorgeous. Various videos and online resources are available to enhance one's fashion sense. First and foremost, understanding what enhances your looks is essential.

Figure-1.1- Structure of Signature Style

- **KNOW YOUR BODY SHAPE AND BODY TYPE:**

All bodies are different, influenced by genetics, gender, diet, and age, resulting in varying body shapes. These can change over time, and it's important to accept and respect this fact. Some may be tall, lean, slim, curvy, short, or petite.

Angelina Jolie, a renowned Hollywood actor, was severely bullied during her childhood for being very lean. However, she's now considered one of the most beautiful women on Earth, exemplified by her Oscar-winning role in "Girl, Interrupted"

(1999). This transformation is just one example of how anyone can achieve their glow-up. Embrace hope, as there's always a ray of sunshine.

God has created human bodies in various forms and shapes, each equally beautiful. Following are the examples:

- Pear-shaped body type: Narrow shoulders with a heavier and bulkier bottom portion, resembling a pear shape. Celebrities like Kim Kardashian and Rihanna have pear-shaped bodies.

- Hourglass-shaped body type: Ideal proportions with upper and lower body measurements nearly equal, and a narrow waist. Examples include Marilyn Monroe, Elizabeth Taylor, and Priyanka Chopra.

- Inverted Triangle body type: Wide shoulders with a narrow bottom portion and a heavier chest area.Examples include Angelina Jolie and Naomi Campbell.

-Rectangle body shape: Shoulders and lower body parts are in equal proportion.Celebrities like Kendall Jenner and Gal Gadot have this body type.

- Oval or apple-shaped body type: Equal measurements at the top and bottom with a heavy stomach area. Oprah winfrey is an example.

-Petite body type: Height of 5ft 4 inches or less,varying in sizes from extra small to triple large, with body shapes including oval, pear-shaped, hourglass, etc.

- **GET A SIGNATURE MAKEUP LOOK:**

Makeup plays an important role in enhancing facial features. It is often used to conceal birthmarks, dark circles, and other imperfections temporarily by using a concealer. Makeup can also boost your mood, and experimenting with different colors can increase your self-esteem. It is not necessary to use makeup on a daily basis; some people prefer a zero-makeup look. It is their choice, and there is nothing wrong with using makeup to enhance your appearance.

Makeup is particularly important in professions like aviation and the beauty and fashion industry, as it can give you a polished look. There are different types of makeup, including bold, minimalist, and no-makeup looks. There are no rigid rules when it comes to doing makeup.

"Simplicity is the keynote of all true elegance", Coco Chanel

Makeup should complement your skin tone; identify your undertone. There are three types of undertone, they are as follows;

1. Warm - When the veins on the wrist appear green in natural light, it indicates warmth in your skin tone. Gold jewellery tends to complement warm undertones better.
2. Cool - When the veins on the wrist appear purple in natural light, it suggests cool undertones. Silver and platinum jewellery are typically more flattering for this type.
3. Neutral - When both green and purple veins are visible on the wrist in natural light, individuals with this undertone are considered fortunate. Most things suit them well.

- **TYPES OF MAKEUP:**

Dewy Makeup:

Oil-based products are used to create a dewy and glossy effect on the face. Lip glosses are preferred over lipsticks. Women with oily skin usually avoid this type of makeup, as it can become messy during hot summers.

No-Makeup Makeup Look:

This is the most trendy makeup style. As the name suggests, the finished look appears as if it is bare skin. The no-makeup look is typically achieved with basic products, such as concealing flaws and using highlighter to give a glossy, natural effect to the skin.

Smokey Makeup:

Smokey eyes are a favourite aspect of eye makeup. A dark-coloured eyeshadow is used to create a smudged and smokey effect, often done for night parties.

Bold Makeup:

Bold makeup involves a dark and colorful theme. Red lipstick paired with different colored metallic eyeshadows is preferred for parties. Experimenting with different colors, such as neons, is common.

Matte Makeup:

This makeup creates no glossiness or shine on the skin; instead, setting powder is used to achieve a dry and matte look. There are products available to help achieve this specific look.

- **METHOD TO DO BASIC MAKEUP:**

Skincare:

Begin by cleansing your face with a face wash, then apply toner and moisturizer according to your skin type.

Primer:

This product smoothens the skin's surface and fills open pores. Various options are available.

Concealer:

Used to hide spots and acne marks, it's a thick cream based product, lighter than your skin tone by only one shade.

Colour Corrector:

Similar to concealer, it hides dark circles, purple skin, or green shades on the face.

Foundation:

Choose a shade matching your skin tone. Various types include liquid, stick, pancake, and serum foundations. This product provides a perfect base for makeup.

Compact:

A lightweight powder is used to set all applied products. Options include loose powder and setting powders; avoid talcum powders. It helps create a matte makeup look.

Eyeliner/Kohl:

Apply on the waterline, lower lash line, and upper lash line. Styles range from bold or winged eyeliner to cat-eye eyeliner.

Different colors of liners are also available, like blue, green, neon, etc.

Mascara:

Applied on eyelashes to add volume and achieve a curled look. Eyelashes can give you a dramatic look, making it the best part of makeup.

Artificial Eyelashes:

Glued to the upper lash line for a dramatic effect; avoid using these at workplaces. They enhance facial features beautifully.

Eyeshadows:

Used to highlight the eyelids using different colors, nude shades for a subtle look, while smokey eyes are best for parties. Various eyeshadow palettes are available to accentuate your eyes.

Contour:

A shade darker than your skin tone for a sculpted, slimmer face. Use proper techniques to avoid looking unnatural.

Blush:

A light pinkish-peach pigment applied to the apples of the cheeks. Cream and powdered blushes are available.

Eyebrow Pencil/Filler:

Used to fill eyebrows to give a perfect shape and fuller appearance. Typically, brown shades are used worldwide.

Lipstick:

Lipsticks come in various shades, including lip gloss, lipstick, lip balms, and lip liners. Red is a bold choice for any occasion, while pink gives a more feminine look. Browns, peaches, and nudes are available according to skin color.

Highlighter:

Adds a beautiful shine to your face when applied on the bridge of the nose and above the blush area. Metallics and glossy illuminators look so beautiful.

Makeup Fixer:

A setting spray to prolong makeup wear and enhance its appearance, providing a flawless finish by laminating the makeup and making it sweatproof.

Makeup Remover:

Choose micellar water for effective and gentle makeup removal, prioritizing skin health. It is the most necessary product for makeup lovers, especially with the availability of waterproof products in the market. Cleansing milks and micellar water are available for thorough removal.

- **SIGNATURE HAIRSTYLE:**

Hair plays an important role in completing a perfect look. Understanding which hairstyle suits you best is essential. Consult a hairstylist to discover your unique style. Different types of hair accessories such as hair clips, clutchers, ribbons, hairpins, and scrunchies can help you achieve a signature style. Hair coloring techniques like highlights, ombre, and lowlights can also add dimension to your look. Avoid highlighting your hair in neon shades to maintain classy look.

A good hairstyle can provide a confidence boost, and people often notice your hair at first sight. Hair should be clean and polished, as it is a crucial part of your overall personality. It is essential to have a good hair care routine. Long hair requires extra care; otherwise, it could ruin your entire look.

1. Wash your hair regularly or maintain a hair washing routine according to your hair type.
2. Choose hair accessories that suit your hair type and the occasion.
3. Apply heat protectant spray before using hair styling devices like hair straighteners, curlers, or clamps.
4. Use hair fixing spray to set your hairstyle.
5. To maintain healthy hair, regular oiling is essential. Use oils like olive oil, coconut oil, almond oil, or mustard oil.
6. Opt for herbal shampoo and conditioner to avoid harsh chemicals in cleansing products.

7. Use a DIY hair mask or packed hair mask once a week to promote healthy, shiny, and silky hair.

- **SIGNATURE ACCESSORIES:**

Different types of accessories can enhance your personal style. Your choice of accessory can add uniqueness to your style and bring spark to a monotonous look. Statement pieces can truly set you apart from others. Choose wisely, keeping your personal style in mind. Experiment and create a versatile style.Avoid excessive spending to achieve an expensive look .Two points should be remember,

- Quality should be prioritized over quantity
- Less is more when it comes to accessorizing.

Few examples are mentioned below:
Handbags:
Black leather handbags always make a statement. Choose your bag according to the occasion; different types are suitable for various purposes, such as tote bags, handbags, clutches, and sling bags..
Scarves:
A silk scarf in different patterns is also a great option for a signature style. You can buy pastels to achieve a classy and elegant look.
Jewellery:
Delicate jewellery, such as gold chains, bracelets, hoop earrings, studs, solitaire rings, bangles, and anklets, are timeless choices. Silver jewellery and dainty pieces are also popular options.
Sunglasses:
They are an important accessory to protect your eyes from UV rays. Opt for polarized glasses for added protection.
Watches:

Watches epitomize elegance and class, making them the perfect gift for anyone.

In addition, hats, hairbands, shawls, brooches, ties, and rings could serve as your statement pieces. Select them according to your profession and vibe. Never make the mistake of copying others; accessorizing can give you a refined look that is uniquely yours.

- **SKIN CARE REGIMEN:**

First step is to know your type:

1. Dry skin – When the skin feels tight after washing, it indicates a lack of moisture. Make sure to understand that there is difference between dry skin and dehydrated skin.
2. Oily skin – When your skin feels sweaty even after washing and produces excess oil, it is more prone to acne.
3. Normal skin – When the skin maintains a balanced moisture level without producing excess oil.
4. Combination skin – When the T-zone of the face (bridge of nose and forehead) is oily and acne-prone, while the rest of the face is dry.
5. Sensitive skin – This indicates very fragile skin that requires gentle care.

Daily Skincare Routine:

1. Cleanser: Wash your face with a gentle face wash tailored to your skin type.
2. Toning: Toning provides nourishment to your skin, closes open pores, and maintains the pH balance of your skin.
3. Moisturizing:This is the most crucial part of the regimen; even those with oily skin need to moisturize.
4. Apply body lotion to make your skin hydrated all day.
5. Maintain hydration in body by drinking water and juices.

Weekly skincare routine:
Follow exfoliation using either gentle exfoliator or chemical exfoliator, once or twice a week. Steam your face for deep cleansing.

Monthly skincare regimen:
Facial and Clean-up: Treat yourself to a facial or clean-up once a month, either at home or at a parlour.

Korean Skincare Routine(Advanced skincare regimen):
Oil Cleanser: Oil cleansers are used to remove makeup and dissolve sebum from the skin.

Water-Based Cleanser: These cleansers are used after oil cleansing to remove all the dirt from the face.

Exfoliator: Different types of exfoliators are used to remove blackheads and whiteheads. The nose and chin areas are more prone to blackheads. Physical exfoliants containing granules can be harsh on the skin and should be used once or twice a week. Sensitive-skinned people should avoid over-exfoliation. Chemical exfoliants, containing acids like alpha hydroxy, beta hydroxy acid peels, and salicylic acid, are also available. They can be used once or twice a week, depending on the skin type. These acids may sound intimidating, but they are gentle on the skin and provide deep exfoliation.

Toner: Toners are used to balance the pH level of the skin, leaving it cleansed and neutralized.

Essence: Essences provide heavy moisturization to the skin.

Ampoule/Serum: Ampoules or serums are used for spot treatment, such as acne marks or pigmentation.

Sheet Mask: Sheet masks are shaped to fit the face and are soaked in a heavy ampoule. They provide hydration to the skin, leaving it glowing.

Eye Cream: Eye creams are used to remove dark circles and reduce under-eye bags.

Moisturizer: These moisturizers are rich in oils and serums, locking in hydration. They are heavy moisturizers.

Sunscreen: Sunscreen must be used to block the sun's rays from damaging your skin.

- **HOMEMADE SKINCARE:**

1. For Cleansing: Add some rosewater to gram flour, apply it for a few minutes, then wash it off with water.
2. For Toning: Apply mint water, cucumber juice, or green tea as a toner.
3. For Moisturizing: Apply aloe vera gel.
4. Face Masks: Apply sandalwood powder for spotless skin, mashed papaya for anti-aging benefits, neem powder mixed with rose water to treat acne and breakouts, and fuller's earth to treat oily skin.

- **NEVER UNDERESTIMATE THE POWER OF THE RIGHT FOOTWEAR:**

Any dress or look can be ruined by the wrong footwear. Use different footwear wisely according to the occasion.

1. For offices, consider wearing pumps, stilettos, or loafers.
2. For casual outings, opt for sneakers or sandals.
3. In my opinion, itis best to avoid crocs and flip-flops. However, if they make you comfortable or set you apart from others, feel free to wear them.
4. Consider high boots, low boots, and heels for classy and elegant look.

"You can be gorgeous at thirty, charming at forty, and irresistible for the rest of your life" Coco Chanel

As stated above, age is just a number. You can start working on your personality at any age. You can be either a working or a non-working individual.

- **IDENTIFY YOUR POWER COLOUR:**

Knowing your power color can be the best advice for looking fabulous all the time. Wear that color more often; there is nothing wrong with repeating either colors or clothes. Wear what you like; life is very short.Understanding the color wheel theory can be daunting, but it's crucial to know that colors have hues such as warm, cool, and neutral.

For a professional appearance, opt for monochromatic ensembles such as blazers, trousers, or skirts that align with your personality. Pay close attention to the fabric, as it plays a crucial role. Avoid sheer clothing in the workplace.

For those who embrace modest fashion, finding suitable attire can be a challenge. Consider full-length skirts, maxi dresses, tunics paired with trousers, and various types of scarves available in both markets and online stores. Many brands worldwide cater to modest dressing needs.Perfectly fitted clothes are essential for a polished look.

"Dress shabbily and they remember the dress; dress impeccably and they remember the woman"-Coco Chanel

- **BALANCED AND HEALTHY DIET:**

A healthy diet is a crucial component of overall well-being, both internally and externally. It's important to follow a balanced diet that includes green vegetables, leafy greens, fruits, dried fruits, nuts, sprouts, juices, meat, eggs, fish, seafood, and dairy products like milk.

For iron-rich foods, consider incorporating beetroot into your diet. Sources of calcium include milk and yogurt, while magnesium-rich foods should also be included in your diet for optimal health. Additionally, prioritize a protein-rich diet to support muscle health and overall wellness.

Drink water at regular intervals and carry a water bottle with you. Replace plain water with infused water, and include juices and smoothies in your diet for better health.

Exercise:

Exercise is an essential component of achieving a physical glow-up. Activities such as swimming, cycling, and running help in maintaining a healthy weight. Do whatever is necessary for your fitness, as this is your life,do it for yourself. Take a 10-minute walk before sleeping. Consider getting a gym membership; don't wait for the new year. Regularly working out can reduce the risk of diseases like diabetes and heart attacks.

Hygiene:

Ensure optimal hygiene by thoroughly cleansing yourself after using the restroom. Regularly bathe and adhere to a consistent hair washing routine. Utilize an intimate cleanser. Periodically remove pubic hair. Maintain cleanliness during menstruation by frequently changing sanitary pads and disposing of them properly. Consider using panty liners for daily discharge. Opt for breathable innerwear. Rinse the genital area with water after each use of the restroom.

Body Language:

Maintaining good posture is crucial. Walk with confidence and avoid slouching while seated, as these actions convey non-verbal communication. Gestures and hand movements can significantly enhance interaction. Refining your body language can foster a strong, positive impression.

- **SUMMARY:**

1. We cannot deny the fact that your outer appearance matters; first impressions are lasting impressions. If your first impression did not go well, then you could work on it. Your style should be versatile, and you can opt for a capsule wardrobe. Your first impression is always based on your appearance, so work on it.To stand out from the crowd, adopt a statement style.
2. Remember to use water after using the restroom and always wash your hands with soap or hand wash afterward. Bath regularly, consider using intimate wash.
3. Maintain good posture; your body language plays an important role.

4. Instead of dressing to impress, focus on dressing to feel good. Try adopting a carefree dressing approach.
5. Ensure your clothes are properly ironed; you can use an iron or steamer.
6. Pay attention to the little details as they can make a significant impact.
7. There are no rigid rules for dressing or accessorizing.
8. However, prioritize maintaining a hygienic, polished look consistently.
9. If your eyesight is not optimal, consider LASIK surgery to remove the need for glasses. While wearing glasses is perfectly fine, LASIK is an option if you prefer not to wear them.
10. It is better to be overdressed than underdressed.
11. Establish a skincare routine for both morning and night. Invest in a good skincare regimen because clear skin can boost your confidence significantly.
12. Consider getting a professional makeover if necessary.
13. Spend money on classic dresses, blazers and high quality accessories.

BE HIGH-VALUE PERSON

"Character is doing the right thing when nobody's looking". J.C. Watts

A highly valued person is the most attractive individual in the room. Loyalty is one of life's highest virtues; you cannot learn loyalty, honesty, generosity, and kindness from books. These qualities are inherent. Purify yourself by removing dishonesty, cheating, and lying from your life. Be loyal to yourself first, then extend that loyalty to relationships and professionally. Be vigilant against negative impulses that may tempt you.Be generous enough to pay bills; don't rely on others. Share expenses or split costs, but avoid being taken advantage of.

Set boundaries in every aspect of life: humor, mental clutter, physical and spiritual associations. Decide what to hold onto and what to discard. Establish who can be part of your inner circle and what behavior you will tolerate or ignore, and take appropriate action when necessary.

Respect yourself and others. Be kind to yourself first, then extend that kindness to others. Practice loyalty to yourself before showing it in your job and relationships. Shine brightly with your personality, and you will inevitably attract envy, rumors, haters, and conspiracies. Above all, prioritize God in your life—God first, then yourself, then others or work. Respect and love God first.

Being generous can break any curses you may face; pay bills, celebrate, and give to charity. If you are at your lowest, rise from the ashes.

Avoid self-praise in front of others, as it can create a negative impression. Let others praise you behind your back; that's true personality. Self-appreciation internally is essential for feeling good about yourself and your accomplishments.

Have depth in your personality; delve into deep topics and engage in profound conversations about stars, nature, the sun, aliens, space, poets, and philosophers. Read psychology to increase your understanding. Explore new places with friends. If you have knowledge, you will be more silent and calm, which will make you stand out from the crowd.

Handle your emotions with shopping therapy, but be cautious as it can become a curse, leading to excessive spending. Instead, buy something budget-friendly that won't break the bank.

Remember little details about others, especially those you care about; this will make you more attractive. Speak softly and fluently, taking small pauses but not overly long ones. Use gap fillers and consider speech therapy if needed. Record your video or audio and listen to it for improvement in improvisation.

Don't be a mood spoiler. When another person is happy or in a good mood, don't get irritated. Instead, be happy and excited for their small victories. If you want to attract happiness into your life, let others live peacefully; don't drain their positive energy by being grumpy or giving them the silent treatment. Avoid ruining their mood by cancelling plans at the last minute.One day, you might find yourself alone without anyone around to celebrate your achievements.

"Understand that everyone is beautiful in their own way. Every skin tone is beautiful. However, not every beautiful person is elegant or classy."

Don't exude desperate energy for anything; your energy or vibe cannot be hidden or faked. When girls become desperate around boys, it's considered one of the worst behaviors they can exhibit. Laughing excessively, being jealous of other girls, and changing one's voice around boys are not classy behaviors. To be classy, strive to balance your personality.

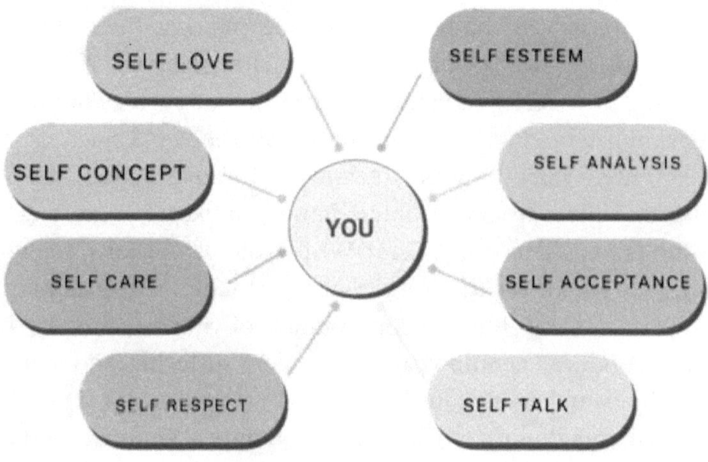

Figure-2.1: Structure of Being You

- **SELF LOVE:**

If you don't love yourself first, you can never love someone else. But if you love yourself too much, you can never love someone else either. We must understand the fundamental law of self-love: it's about taking care of yourself first, then extending that care to others. It's essential not to misinterpret self-love as self-priority or self-respect. Never disrespect others in the name of self-love.

When you feel disrespected by anyone or in any situation, simply walk away without explanation,they likely already know. Self-respect is an extension of self-love. It means respecting yourself enough to prioritize meals, take breaks, indulge in self-care activities like spa treatments or sports, and to leave situations or relationships when necessary. Stand up for yourself without causing harm to others.

- **NEVER TAKE ADVANTAGE OF ILLNESS:**

I have observed many individuals exploiting their illness to avoid work or social engagements with friends. If you are employing this strategy to shirk responsibilities such as homework, studies, household chores, or duties at the workplace, it may inadvertently hurt others' feelings. Moreover, this deceitful behaviour will eventually rebound upon you like a boomerang.

Who are you deceiving, God? While you may deceive the entire world, only He knows the truth. You might achieve your aspirations through dishonesty, but as a consequence of your falsehoods, those who have endured genuine hardships, silent suffering, and tears will eventually overshadow your life.

"Dreams don't have an expiration date"- Shahrukh khan

- **LOOKISM:**

Pretty Privilege is a tangible phenomenon. Our society is significantly biased towards physical appearance. Fair skin, sharp features, and a lean physique are often deemed the pinnacle of attractiveness. This bias is deeply rooted in the pervasive influence of media in our daily lives. Media perpetuates colourism and racism unabashedly. Individuals who do not conform to these arbitrary beauty standards frequently suffer from mental health issues, including low self-esteem and depression. The implications for relationships are particularly concerning. It is undeniable that preferential treatment is often accorded to aesthetically pleasing individuals, functioning like a premium code for those deemed attractive. This form of discrimination must be eradicated, and a shift towards accepting individuals for who they are is imperative.

- **CHARISMA:**

Charisma encompasses attractiveness, magnetism, elegance, social etiquette, kindness, empathy, and a genuinely classy personality. To be charismatic, self-acceptance is key. Embrace your skin color, hair type, and physical appearance; only then can others appreciate your true beauty and charm.

Confidence is a crucial factor. Confidence arises from being authentic and not succumbing to jealousy or pretense. Your body language should be so poised and attractive that it doesn't convey desperation or insecurity. Maintain a straight posture, and walk with assurance. Developing strong communication skills is essential: be a good listener, and avoid interrupting others while they speak.

Looks alone are insufficient to be charismatic. Cultivate empathy towards others, genuinely feel their emotions, and avoid spoiling the mood by imposing your feelings on them. Build rapport in the workplace. Exhibit a positive attitude, light humor, and optimism. Smile often and maintain good eye contact during conversations.

Avoid being bossy; instead, aim to be a good leader. Adopt admirable characteristics, and develop networking skills. When meeting someone, greet them with respect and kindness. These qualities can be nurtured through practice and consistency. A charismatic person is truly irresistible.

The emotional quotient (EQ) is a crucial factor in both personal and professional development. This term, popularized by Daniel Goleman in his book, *Emotional Intelligence: Why It Can Matter More Than IQ*, highlights the importance of managing emotions through understanding one's own weaknesses, strengths, and values. Acknowledging feelings is essential.

These qualities aid in building a cohesive team in the workplace and fostering a strong rapport with others. Understanding and empathizing with the emotions of others can significantly enhance interpersonal relationships and professional success.

Avoid excessive laughter, as it undermines the impression of class and elegance. While it's fine to share a good laugh with close friends, refrain from engaging in inappropriate behavior in restaurants and meetings, as it can tarnish your reputation. Refrain from eating during meetings. Offer gifts without expecting anything in return. Avoid self-obsession and strive for balance in your demeanour.

• **UNDERSTAND PERSONALITIES:**

Understanding personalities based on introversion, extroversion, and ambiversion can significantly impact your relationships and professional interactions. Introverts are often mischaracterized as shy and socially awkward, which is a complete myth; they simply need alone time to organize their thoughts. Extroverts gain energy from social gatherings and are often perceived as bold and confident. However, ambiverts possess traits of both extroversion and introversion, requiring time to balance these tendencies.

Respect all personality traits; no one is inherently better than another. Instead of trying to change others, strive to understand them.

• **WHAT TO CARRY IN HANDBAG:**

A genuinely classy individual never relies on others for basic necessities. It's wise to maintain a travel-friendly kit containing your own makeup, sanitary products, medications, and first aid essentials.

1. Sanitiser
2. Makeup- lipgloss, or whatever you like
3. Sunscreen
4. Sunglasses
5. Keys/money/cards
6. Mobile phone
7. Nuts/dry berries/ chocolates

8. Mouth wash
9. Pen and diary
10. Comb or hairbrush
11. Moisturiser

- **SUMMARY:**

1. There's a fine line between confidence and overconfidence.
2. Ensure that your self-love doesn't lead you down the path of narcissism.
3. Consider others' emotions; don't be mean.
4. Mental health is as important as physical health.
5. First and foremost, be honest with yourself and conduct a self-analysis of your behavior.
6. Start reading books and learning new things.
7. There will always be setbacks; you are not on this earth to live a perfect, heavenly life.
8. Keep your morals high, forgive others, and understand that it's not necessary to keep them in your life forever.
9. Acceptance is the foundation of a high-vibration lifestyle. Accept your physical attributes as granted by the Almighty, while maintaining hygiene and other practices discussed in Chapter 1.
10. Embrace God's role in every situation, whether it's a setback or anything else; it is always God's will.
11. If you want others to admire you, outer beauty alone is not enough.
12. Maintain awareness of your mood, decisions, and responses.
13. Be mindful of the words that come out of your mouth.
14. Strive to be a person of integrity; people will be irresistibly drawn to you.
15. Take note that it's not just about being noticed but being remembered.
16. Aim to become highly valued, just as you work on your physical appearance or earning money.

17. Keeping good company is a blessing. If you find one, cherish it. Do not betray your friends. Never chase after people.
18. A real woman supports other women.
19. Avoid harbouring hatred towards men.
20. Don't make yourself too readily available to men.
21. Be faithful to your partner.
22. To comprehend this concept fully, it is essential to maintain proper hygiene and a keen sense of style. Educate yourself, and cultivate refined etiquette.
23. These qualities aid in building a cohesive team in the workplace and fostering a strong rapport with others. Understanding and empathizing with the emotions of others can significantly enhance interpersonal relationships and professional success.Outer beauty is not sufficient for a strong personality; work on your inner well-being. Maintain high morals.
24. Never let your inner child to die.
25. Maintain innocence and cheerfulness in your personality.
26. Take a personality test from online websites to know yourself better.
27. Never lower down your standards to keep your friendship or relationship.
28. Don't cancel plan in last moment.
29. Always be on time.
30. Don't respond to mean comments. Just ignore.
31. Your true character shows when you have everything in your life.
32. Learn to say no, when needed. Stop being people pleaser.

CHAPTER THREE

CHANGE THE PARADIGM OF YOUR LIFE

In this life, when we find ourselves stuck in particular patterns of behaviour and reactions to different situations, these patterns hinder our personal development. To change this paradigm for personal transformation and to find purpose and satisfaction in life, we need to understand the underlying patterns.

We must become aware of our beliefs and their outcomes. Recognizing our patterns and reactions to certain situations allows us to break free from stagnant patterns and repeated cycles in relationships and careers.

Being open to changing our mindset and thought processes is essential. Firstly, we should identify the beliefs ingrained in our minds. Change may make us uncomfortable, but it's important to accept it and adapt to different patterns with a new mindset. Embrace chaos and failure by accepting the situation.

Transforming bad habits into good ones is crucial. Being disciplined towards our goals and showing kindness towards others are important aspects of this process.

Microhabits can alter the course of our lives towards a successful and growth-oriented mindset. Incorporating gratitude into our lives, acknowledging small wins, and not losing hope during setbacks are vital practices. Understanding that setbacks are part of life's journey and shifting our thoughts from negative to positive affirmations helps us gracefully embrace the journey.

The power of transformation lies within us because humans are created in such a way by God.

- **BELIEFS:**

Superstition is often the culprit behind setbacks, whether it's a bird perched on your door or a cat crossing your path. When we become trapped in fixed patterns of behaviour and reactions to various situations, our personal development stagnates. To break free from this cycle and achieve personal transformation, we must understand our paradigms.

Awareness of our beliefs and their consequences is crucial. Recognizing our patterns and reactions allows us to break free from repetitive cycles in relationships and careers. We must be open to changing our mindset and thought processes, identifying and challenging the beliefs ingrained in our minds.

Change can be uncomfortable, but accepting it is the first step. Embrace different mindsets, adapt to new patterns, and welcome chaos and failure as part of the journey. Transform negative habits into positive ones, cultivate discipline towards your goals, and show kindness to others.

Shift your focus from negativity to positive affirmations. Life is a journey with inevitable ups and downs, embrace it gracefully. Remember, the power of transformation lies within us, as we are intricately designed by a higher power.

- **EXPECTATIONS:**

Have realistic expectations for yourself and others. Be mindful of your demands and expect nothing from others, not even from your parents or spouse. Instead, place your expectations in God, as God is capable of achieving the impossible. Have high expectations of God. Expecting things from others could shatter your soul.

- **BREAK THE PATTERN:**

Intentionally change your responses, patterns, likes, and dislikes.

1. Analyze the patterns and repeated cycles in your life, identifying areas where you feel stuck.
2. Repeated habits and reactions can create a spiral effect in similar situations.
3. Instead of dwelling on events, begin building a new framework by changing small habits.
4. Sometimes, deliberately altering your responses can significantly impact outcomes. When triggered by hidden traumas, choose a different response—stop reacting and start responding.
5. Evaluate your friendships and declutter your contact list. Understanding the context behind every response is key to growth.
6. Seek to understand the underlying situations behind every response.
7. Consider changing your friend circle and decluttering your contact list

"If you aren't charged up about doing something, if you don't have what in Hindi we call the 'Josh', the fire in your belly for it, then don't do it."- Shahrukh khan

- **BURNT TOAST THEORY:**

BURNT TOAST THEORY

Figure-3.1: Burnt Toast Theory

The Burnt Toast Theory states that minor inconveniences can lead to unexpected positive outcomes. Imagine the disappointment of burning toast in the morning and needing an extra ten minutes to make a new one. This delay could shape our day or have a beneficial impact. Even small mishaps can bring us good moments and peace. Minor misfortunes are part of life's unpredictable journey, and these setbacks can have a ripple effect, leading to unexpected benefits if we try to understand the reasons behind them.

This theory can literally change mindsets and significantly impact personal growth. It can help us live a balanced life. Delays are a part of life and could prevent major accidents. Sometimes these mishaps disrupt our daily routines, like spilling tea on a dress, missing a bus, or burning toast. Adopting this mindset provides an optimistic outlook on life. This theory brings us closer to the idea that a higher power is planning everything for us.

To understand and apply this concept, reframe bad situations in your mind with a positive outcome. There is always beauty in chaos. Try to see the beauty in chaos and understand that minor delays and setbacks are not negative. In other words, we can say this theory embraces the idea of a "blessed mess." Sometimes a mess can lead to the opening of closed doors. A wrong turn may lead you to meeting your soulmate.

- **TOXIC POSITIVITY:**

Toxic positivity refers to the act of forcing positivity while suppressing negative emotions. This practice is extremely dangerous for mental health. When emotions are deeply suppressed, it can lead to mental illness. To be authentic, negative emotions should be managed properly. No one can lead a truly positive life all the time, and a perfect life doesn't exist. It's important to maintain balanced emotions and channel negative feelings calmly. Additionally, one must understand that crying is not a sign of weakness. In fact, crying can effectively release stress.

Schedule appointments with a dentist, psychiatrist for mental health, therapist, and dermatologist if needed. There is no shame in seeking professional help. Visit skincare clinics for facials, manicures, and pedicures if your budget allows.

CHANGE...CHANGE...CHANGE:

Transform your reality by observing patterns. Sometimes, physical change alone isn't sufficient; change your mindset. Alter your perfume, keychain, wallpaper, route, thoughts, usual food orders, coffee mug, and dress for an instant mood lift. Change the color of your room's walls.Keep a diary and a pen handy, and keep your mind open to new possibilities.

Engage in your favorite activities, but don't impose them on others. Everything begins with your thought process.Avoid multitasking too much. Live and work in a simple and smooth manner.

Show appreciation for your work; share it with everyone except those who don't appreciate it.Time will fix things; let things unfold naturally. Don't sit idle; work on improving yourself. Patterns can be broken by shifting your energy and mindset.Changing the overall process takes time.

Handle silent haters and envious people around you with kindness and calmness. Don't panic; initially, try to avoid them by ignoring their negativity. Be assertive and address any issues directly if needed. As you become more attractive and magnetic, you may attract more haters and envious individuals. Learn to manage them; this is akin to celebrity energy.

- **SUMMARY:**

1. The ability to change ourselves lies within us.
2. Unlock your better version by changing microhabits.
3. Repeated behaviors are a sign of being stuck.
4. Patterns will persist until you change yourself or learn the lesson.
5. Changing small things can create a butterfly effect in your life.
6. Stop dwelling in the past. Let your future shine so brightly that nobody can dim it.
7. Delays are a part of life; there is always good hidden behind delays.
8. Embrace failure as a victory because you have tried.
9. There is beauty in chaos.
10. Let go of all superstitions and have complete faith in the Almighty.
11. Unleash your feminine or masculine energy by altering your thought process.
12. Start journaling.
13. Transformation includes physical, mental, and spiritual changes.
14. Once you start transforming, you will begin noticing coincidences and surprises.

CHAPTER FOUR

LIVE AN AESTHETIC LIFE

Enjoy your life as if it is the masterpiece of God. Cherish every moment and practice patience during difficult times. Shift your mindset. Decorate your living space, work desk, and kitchen counter with rice lights, ribbons, stickers, motivational quotes, plants, or anything else you fancy. Avoid overspending on materialistic things; instead, focus on shifting your mindset towards a more fulfilling way of life. Strive to maintain peace in your mind, body, and soul,this is the essence of aesthetic living.

- **PRIORITIES:**

Prioritize your life, recognizing that you cannot treat everyone on the same scale. Prioritizing can clarify your vision regarding career, health, and relationships. It can simplify your job, making it easier. Effective prioritization aids in time and financial management. Categorize your tasks into different sections such as health, relationships, friendships, career, job, family, and self-care. Use to-do lists, calendars, and apps to schedule your tasks. Apply the Eisenhower Matrix to categorize tasks and distinguish between urgent and important ones. This approach helps build a harmonious balance between personal and external life.

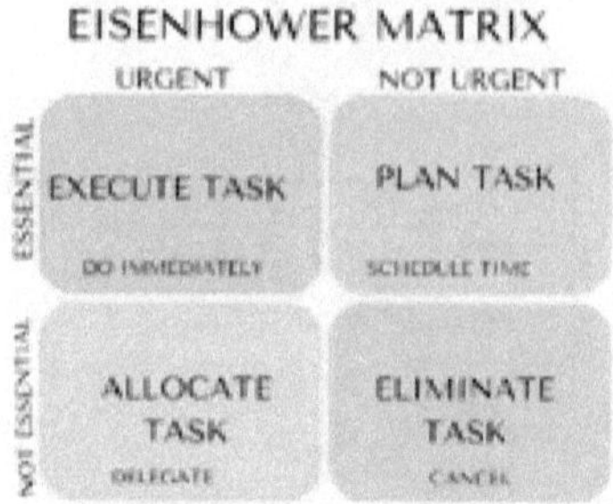

Figure-4.1: Eisenhower Matrix Structure

- **ROMANTICISE YOUR LIFE:**

Smiling improves mood, as researched by scientists. Maintaining your mood can be challenging; you can't always be happy and may fluctuate between different emotional states. However, faking a smile until you genuinely feel better is a proven method supported by science.

Figure-4.2: Romanticise Life

Beautify your life by romanticizing it; enjoy the rain and the breeze. Find creativity in every aspect of life and take pleasure in everything happening around you. Add a theme to your workspace or room, creating a cozy nook that reflects your creativity. Embrace your uniqueness with sophistication and add colors to your life.

You have the choice between minimalist, artistic, or vibrant interiors. Aim to enrich your life by noticing beauty in everything. Unleash the artist within you and avoid spending too much money on unnecessary things. Instead, create your own art through DIY projects.

Ultimately, all we seek is mental peace and the beauty around us. You can start by incorporating fragrances, candles, books, and lamps into your life. Explore handicraft galleries, antiques stores, museums, and art galleries. Appreciate the simplicity of the moon, the warmth of sunlight, and the velvety touch of flowers. Be the living poem and preserve dried flowers as souvenirs.

Start giving thoughtful gifts to family, friends, teachers, and loved ones to make them feel special. Eradicate any superstitions you may have and express yourself through painting and poetry. Love others as they are and avoid trying to change them. Instead, become the change you wish to see.

Show appreciation for patterns, textures, and beauty in everyday life. Remember, if you don't love yourself, you can't love others. Speak delicately with warmth and elegance, expanding your vocabulary with aesthetic words. Little makeup can enhance your beauty, so play with colors as discussed in Chapter 1.

Extend kindness to stray animals and play with children. Declutter your physical and mental space by organizing your belongings and thoughts. Journaling, maintaining a diary, or tracking your routine with an app can help declutter your mind. Meditation can also aid in clearing your thoughts, though it may be challenging.

Living an aesthetic life is a mindset, so avoid being overly materialistic and appreciate what you already have. Enjoy the simple pleasures of life, such as rain, wind, and sunshine, and consider starting collections of items like coins or stamps. Show empathy towards others and avoid expecting too much from them. Remember, you can't build a perfect life on Earth, but you can find beauty in imperfection. Best believe that beauty lies in the eye of the beholder.

Behave like the main character, dress like your favorite movie star, and do silly things that don't harm others. Embrace your weirdness and, above all, be real and authentic. Appreciate other people's aesthetics too. Treat yourself to a solo date, visit bookstores, and get a library membership card. Don't wait for the perfect moment; create high vibes to make the moment perfect. Travel with friends, explore different places, and create lasting memories. Challenge yourself by changing your accent, learning a new language, and indulging in cute finds.

- **UNDERSTAND THE VIBES:**

The term "vibe" originates from vibrations, denoting the energy that surrounds a place, person, or environment. It encompasses a sense of intuition and the emotions associated with various situations, influenced by the ambient energy. Vibes can range from positive and uplifting to negative, toxic, weary, dim, or awakened. For instance, if a room exudes a peaceful vibe, it signifies a tranquil and relaxing atmosphere. Individuals can sense your vibe merely through your presence, establishing a subconscious connection. Different individuals might perceive different vibes in the same setting or from the same person, highlighting the subjective nature of this phenomenon. It is an inherent ability to sense another person's aura. Vibes can profoundly impact our moods and emotions, guiding us toward better decision-making.

While there are no concrete experiments to delineate a good vibe from a bad one, their influence on our lives is undeniably powerful. Vibes are inherently subjective, depending on our perception of a situation or energy. Some people are exceptionally sensitive to toxic vibes and can swiftly detect negative energies. Vibes can also be neutral, neither positively nor negatively charged. Cultivating positive energy equates to fostering a good vibe. For example, plants are often associated with positive vibes, but a tree might evoke fear at night, indicating a perceived negative vibe.

Enhancing your vibes can make you more magnetic. This is a transformative aspect of personal magnetism. Once you analyze and understand your own vibe, you can work on making it more positive. Being truthful invariably brings more positivity; having good intentions generates a positive vibe. Surrounding yourself with plants can also contribute positively. Vibes are the energy one emanates; external beauty can be overshadowed by toxic vibes. This concept transcends materialism and pertains to energies and vibrations.

You can alter the aura around you through practices like meditation, prayer, and communicating with a higher power about your challenges. Avoid incessantly complaining about your problems, as a victim mindset can attract negative vibes. Embracing positivity and striving to maintain a harmonious energy can significantly enhance your overall well-being.

- **ANALYZE THE HEALED AURA:**

A healed aura signifies good health and alignment with your higher self. You generate positive vibes and remain calm in every situation. You don't suppress your emotions; if you need to cry, you allow yourself to do so because crying doesn't make you any less human. You manage anger effectively and express your emotions appropriately. You handle mood swings well, organize your thoughts, trust your intuition, and enhance your gut feelings. Spiritually, you are strong enough to differentiate between negative and positive energies. You have discovered your life's purpose and are actively working on personal growth. Your healed aura creates an energy field that attracts good people around you.

- **FRENEMIES:**

Be wary of frenemies; they will never leave you and will drain your energy like parasites feeding on your soul. Take strong action and cut ties with them immediately. Watch for signs; they rarely reveal their true colors. This will eventually help declutter your friend circle. Only befriend those who align with your values.

When you shine too brightly, others may try to dim your light. Pay them no mind, for where attention goes, energy flows. They may attack your thoughts, spread rumors, assassinate your character, throw shade, and undermine your self-esteem. They may give you bad advice, show a sweet side to stay in your circle, envy you, ask for money, or borrow your things, anything to hurt you. Don't let them into your life. Trust your intuition; this applies not only to relationships but also to workplaces and family gatherings.

If you're the main character, there will inevitably be villains. Prepare yourself to handle them and use these experiences to grow. Give yourself the time you need.

• FLOWERS THERAPY:

Collect flowers and press them in books. Use them to decorate your workplace; they will always be there for you when everyone else leaves you alone. Scrapbook with these flowers to create memories. If nobody gives you flowers, start giving them to others; blessings will follow.

The aesthetic becomes profoundly poetic and inherently natural when flowers are revered. They should be treated with respect, avoid crushing them underfoot or causing harm. Beyond their beauty, flowers offer significant benefits for skincare and healthcare. Embrace their essence by adorning yourself with flower tiaras and bracelets. Remember, flowers are not just adornments; they are our companions in nature. Express your affection and consideration by gifting flowers to others.

• SPIRIT ANIMAL TRICK:

This is a strategy to deal with any person: decode their behavior and understand their pattern of responses. Then relate these attributes to an animal that represents their spirit. That is their spirit animal. Act accordingly based on this understanding. If the person is innocent, their spirit animal could be a bunny. If someone is prone to using poisonous words, their spirit animal might be a snake, you should be cautious not to get "bitten" by them. Some people might be wolves, lions, pandas, or tortoises. This tactic will help you navigate interactions with different types of people.

• SOME TIPS:

Create a positive environment and atmosphere to foster better interactions. Apply perfume or scented lotion.Write something, even if it's just a text or emoji to a friend.Change your display picture on social media, but avoid using it as a signal to broadcast your sadness to everyone. Post appropriate content on social media, such as funny or motivational posts. This might sound funny, but create a time capsule and put all your important and favorite items inside it. You don't have to bury it in the ground; place it somewhere in your house where it isn't easily visible. Then, start collecting memories and creating cherished moments to fill it.Start a scrapbook by pasting your favorite photos and memories. This will help you feel more organized and uplifted.Begin a habit of gifting, as it can create a sense of closeness with others and foster good relationships.Customize items like bottles, pens, t-shirts, and bags to promote self-love.

- **SUMMARY**

1. Avoid being a mood spoiler and try to maintain a positive aura.
2. Eat something you enjoy, as taste can affect mood.
3. Accomplish a small task, like household chores.
4. Keep your desk organized and decorate it with colorful stationary.
5. Talk to a non-toxic friend on the phone or spend time alone if necessary.
6. Seek natural light, either sunlight or moonlight.
7. Avoid listening to music that triggers negative memories.
8. Engage in physical activity like exercise or spending time with pets.
9. Reflect on the root cause of your mood and take steps to address it.
10. Remember that you have the power to change your mood. Stay positive and avoid being grumpy.
11. Consider ordering something online, as receiving a parcel can boost your mood on a bad day.

12. Read good books in your preferred genre.
13. Remove fears from your mind and prioritize gratitude above all else. Being grateful is a choice.
14. Find your aesthetic and adhere to it.
15. Romanticize your life. Vibe is everything.
16. Love God.
17. Love yourself.
18. Love your family and friends.
19. Love your job or work. Remember, God always comes first. Gratitude for the life you have is essential, as many people aspire to live the life you lead.
20. Beautify yourself by wearing clean clothes and makeup.
21. Beautify your surroundings with different colors on walls, artwork, lights, lamps, and elements of nature.
22. Cultivate creativity through activities like painting, writing, music, or any other form of expression. Spread positivity and maintain a positive mindset.
23. Surround yourself with good company,people who embody values like honesty and loyalty.
24. Spend time in nature, engaging in outdoor activities, playing sports, and observing the beauty of flora and fauna.
25. Practice gratitude daily, acknowledging the blessings in your life.
26. Seek diverse experiences to enrich your life.
27. Find purpose in your existence.

CHAPTER FIVE

THE POWER OF CHARITY

"Smiling is a form of charity."- Prophet Muhammad

This chapter will explore the power of charity and how embracing the art of giving can make the world a more peaceful place. It provides comprehensive information about the power of giving.

Charity can take various forms, all of which are selfless acts. Financial charity involves giving money to the poor, needy individuals, or NGOs. Materialistic charity includes donating old books, clothes, and food to those in need.

Offering a helping hand through volunteering at NGOs or participating in community cleaning processes is another form of charity. Charity manifests in numerous ways.

Peter Marshall emphasized, "The measure of life is not its duration, but its donation."

You should be grateful to God for blessing you with the ability to help others. Start by donating even a small amount, like one dollar, daily. Consistency is key, as God loves those who are consistent in their actions.Take small actions, like putting out water for birds and nuts for animals. Carry packets of chocolates or cookies to share with poor children whenever you come across them.

"We make a living by what we get, but we make a life by what we give."-Winston Churchill

Do these acts deliberately to bring positive change to your current situation, whether it's financial or in your love life. Help others without any conditions attached, as conditional help is not true help.Stop judging people based on race, color, ethnicity, or religious beliefs. This will promote mental peace and ultimately make you a better human being.Serve the poor, offer free tuition, and provide counseling. Kindness is the solution to the harshness and cruelty of the world. It's a real superpower that can transform lives.

Stop living a fake life and refrain from sharing your acts of charity online for validation. Instead, donate clothes after washing and ironing them, and add some fragrance for freshness.Consider adopting an animal from a national park and regularly visit NGOs and orphanages. Build friendships with orphans, as they need love and affection the most.

Avoid engaging in negative practices and focus on spreading positivity. Create blessing bags containing essential items like water bottles, sanitary napkins, tissue rolls, chapstick, toothbrush, and toothpaste to distribute to those in need.

Finally, always show respect and offer a smile to others. These small gestures can make a big difference in someone's day.

"The best thing to do with the best things in life is to give them away."-Dorothy Day

- **UNVEIL GOOD INTENTIONS:**

Having crystal clear, good intentions towards others brings more positivity into life. Your vibe can become truly magnetic, fostering virtues like empathy and kindness. Changing your intentions can transform your current situation, shift your reality, and bring satisfaction to your life. It can provide a lasting legacy through good thoughts and can lead to success in your profession. Your relationships can bloom like flowers when you have good intentions towards your partner. Decision-making becomes much easier when you avoid betraying anyone, cheating your partner, or scamming money. This purity of soul is profound.While having good intentions is easy, acting on them is the real challenge. Celebrate others' successes, as jealousy and envious behavior can destroy your magnetic field. Your vibe can become toxic when your intentions are tainted with negative thoughts. Strive to be as clear as clean water so that when people see or approach you, they feel the calmness and coolness in your personality. This is how people will never forget you. Your kindness or advice during difficult times can make your personality incredibly magnetic.

The highest form of help is charity, without any conditions attached,just unconditional assistance. If you want to heal yourself, start donating your favorite food and clothes; this will eventually create good vibrations in your life.

After a breakup, engage in regular charity work. Help impoverished couples with their weddings. If you're experiencing heartbreak, visit orphanages and gift them cute items.If you're unemployed, consider giving grains to birds or providing water for animals.

Goals and actions are necessary. Begin planning accordingly. Start journaling daily to organize your thoughts. If you're feeling stuck, breaking the pattern is the toughest part. Do it intentionally; planners could help you become more disciplined. There are many applications available for self-improvement.Charity makes the plans happen. Before embarking on something significant, donate.

Charity enhances your kindness and generosity, eventually cultivating a positive and magnetic vibe. Giving is intrinsic to humanity; offering good advice and supporting social issues are integral parts of this generosity.

Charity makes you beautiful inside and out. If you seek inner glow, start donating. Charity will give you a brighter appearance. If you seek inner peace, begin giving. If you wish to combat bad luck, increase your giving. The amount should be enough to burn a hole in your pocket. Relax, as God will return it to you tenfold. Your doors will open in unimaginable ways. Your lost things will be found, and your broken heart will begin to heal. Charity prevents bad things from happening.

As Anne Frank once said, "No one has ever become poor by giving."

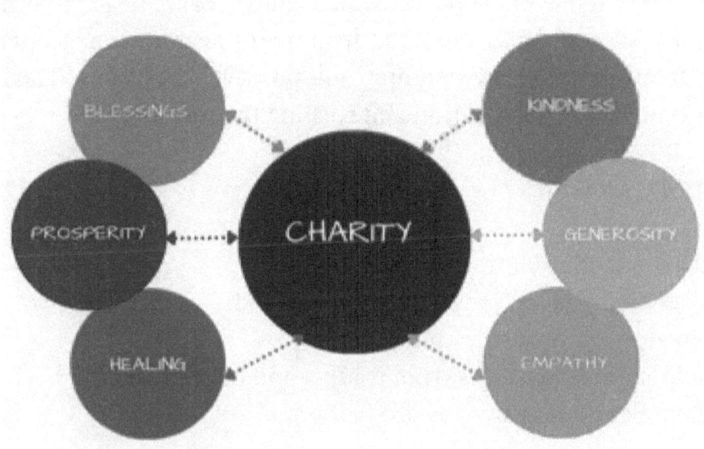

Figure-5.1: Charity Outcomes

- **HELP IN HEALING OTHERS:**

To heal yourself, try to heal others. Show empathy and kindness without absorbing their negative energy. Be discerning about who is genuine. Don't automatically believe someone's tears, as they might be crocodile tears intended to gain your sympathy. Be cautious and investigate situations before trusting anyone.

Heal others with your words. Assist in treatments. Encourage others to fulfill their dreams. Heal through your presence and aura. Spread positivity to those around you. Heal through eye contact. Everyone is broken in different ways. You never know how your smile or a single word can transform someone else's life in beautiful ways. It's true that crushes can have a subconscious healing effect. Whether it's a work crush, school crush, or any crush in general, you might unknowingly be helping someone heal just by being present. Respect the impact you have on others.

Heal yourself by praying for yourself and for others. Support good things and avoid supporting bad things. Bring peace to others to heal your soul, your boss and teammates also need peace. Heal your fractured vibe by sending out positive intentions. Healing takes time; avoid desperation and rushing the process.

- **SUMMARY:**

1. Charity is the solution to all problems.
2. By giving, you are seeking help from God.
3. Donate your favourite things.
4. Help in healing others from trauma and heartbreak.
5. Have clear intentions towards others.
6. Don't be desperate or in a rush.
7. Don't expect others to give back to you; instead, expect from God.
8. Heal with your words.
9. The effect of a crush is real; they help us heal.
10. You might be healing someone just by existing.
11. Become a volunteer in an NGO.

TRUST IN DIVINE TIMING

"Time is the wisest counselor of all."- Pericles

Time is the greatest healer. To understand this concept, we can think of time as the most powerful medicine for our problems. When things are not going according to plan, trust in the process and leave it to a higher power. Be patient while having trust in yourself.

Every therapy requires time to become effective. Maintaining a good habit also takes time to build. By letting go of the situation that is bothering you, your perspective may change. You may gain different insights and develop a new mindset. As time flies, things fade, which can be either good or bad, because good times change just as bad times do.

Time also introduces us to new people and helps us form new connections through networking, which can expand our social circle.

Figure- 6.1: Divine Time

- **THE STORY OF CHINESE BAMBOO TREE:**

If you haven't heard about the Chinese bamboo tree, let me enlighten you. When a bamboo seed is planted in the soil, it does not sprout for five years. However, after those five years, it rapidly grows to a towering height of 90 feet within just five weeks. This remarkable phenomenon teaches us the value of patience and demonstrates that divine timing is at work in our lives.The farmer's faith and patience in watering the seed for five years without expecting immediate results are commendable. Similarly, the lives of some people mirror the journey of the bamboo tree. They may take years to show progress, but once they begin to grow, the wait proves to be worthwhile.

"In the grand scheme of life, every delay is a lesson in divine timing."-Anonymous

For the treatment of mental health issues, therapies require time to show positive results. There is no instant cure for a broken heart; it needs time to heal. The duration depends on the sensitivity of the person. To process any emotion or understand any situation, take your time.

Let go and surrender yourself. Surrendering is not accepting failure, but rather, it means you have strong enough faith to let a higher power do his work.

It is important to note that time alone is not the healer. Medicine needs time to work, and therapies require time to be effective. In cases like a road accident, immediate first aid is necessary; we cannot say that time alone will heal you. After receiving medical treatment, the trauma from the accident will heal or fade slowly, and this healing process requires time.

"The two most powerful warriors are patience and time".
-Leo Tolstoy

- **LAW OF ASSUMPTION:**

It states that your beliefs and thoughts can define your destiny by manifesting what you imagine and expect. Your reality is defined by your inner thoughts. To simulate this concept, feel as though your wish has already been fulfilled. Your assumptions shape your reality. Affirmations and visualization can transform your life. Maintaining consistency in expecting good things and having positive thoughts is the key to this process. Positive self-talk can help build the future you desire so desperately.

- **ADD TO CART THERAPY:**

When you don't know what to do during waiting time,create a comprehensive wishlist by adding all your desired items to the list, and then pray to God for their provision. Don't hesitate, give it a try when you're feeling upset. This practice will strengthen your faith in God. The beauty of it is that you don't know what lies ahead.

Adopt a zero-waste mindset by protecting the environment, saving water, avoiding wastefulness, saving money, and maintaining cleanliness in your surroundings. Refrain from smoking, using drugs, and littering.

Organize your days, months, and year with a routine and timetable. Understand that while you may deviate from your schedule,because everyone plans, but God also plans, no one schedules events like COVID or an apocalypse, nor adds accidents or tragedies. However, preparation is crucial. Lay out your clothes the night before each day and plan your day in advance to minimize stress. Don't save your best clothes for special occasions; use them regularly. You never know what tomorrow may bring.

Don't curse your timing. You are exactly where you need to be. Good times and bad times follow each other; time always changes. So, don't let any heartbreak shatter your soul. The ache inside your heart can feel as real as losing a limb without anesthesia.

Time heals; let things go and allow God to work. Don't interfere; focus on improving yourself. Stop obsessing over your age and comparing yourself to others and your friends. Comparison kills your will to live; you'll never achieve a perfect life, so surrender to the present. You may be moving towards your right time to meet the right person at the right place. The idea of being in the wrong place with the wrong person is an illusion. Every piece will fall into the right place, just as different plants need different times and timelines to ripen.

"Lost time is never found again".- Benjamin Franklin

Time cannot be bought, stopped, stored, or brought back. It is the most powerful asset in the world. Time is a precious currency that cannot be borrowed. Aging is inevitable, so it is important to respect others' time. You can change your timeline by shifting the energies in your mind. Don't waste your time arguing over silly topics or getting involved in others' conflicts. Instead, invest your time in learning and doing something positive. Give time to your family and friends.

Time is unpredictable; anything can happen at any moment. You never know what time will bring, so it's better to expect good things from God and prepare for challenging times. Accept reality and understand that you can rebuild yourself after difficult periods. Time is precious; use it wisely.

- **SUMMARY:**

1. Anything can happen at any time.
2. Time is always defined by God; stop cluttering your mind with other thoughts.
3. Time is the greatest healer.
4. Let go of control and start accepting where you are and what you are.
5. Don't try to manipulate God's plan by indulging in overthinking.
6. There is always a lesson in every setback or redirection provided by God.
7. Reframe the current situation by understanding the lesson or by changing your response; this will gradually change your paradigm too.
8. Everything happens for a particular reason.
9. The outcome might be different from what you are expecting, but there will always be peace, whether it is about marriage, job, or any soul-sucking experience.
10. Your journey will unfold with time intervals as destined by God. Don't stop asking for good things from God.
11. All it takes is faith. Build faith in God first, then trust yourself too.
12. Change your self-concept; if you are not positive with yourself, how could you expect positive circumstances?
13. Once you start shifting your mindset towards divine timing and more gratitude, your life will change drastically.
14. As Steve Jobs said, the dots will always connect once you look back.

15. Start looking for synchronicities when you believe in divine connections and divine time.

CHAPTER SEVEN

MIRACLES DO HAPPEN

"Each moment of worry, anxiety, or stress represents lack of faith in miracles, for they never cease."-T.F. Hodge

Overall, a human being is nothing without God, and possessing patience and a grateful nature can lead you to witness miracles. Miracles occurred with prophets due to their unshakeable faith in God and their gratitude during setbacks. Once you reach this point in life, you will start experiencing miracles. Begin by noting down tiny coincidences, like meeting an old friend in a grocery aisle or receiving unexpected advice. When you find purpose in living, you will feel more grateful, even if you don't have your dream car. You will start experiencing God's hand in everything you do and receive surprises from friends and family. Miracles can include healing from chronic illness or recovering from life-threatening accidents. You may begin to feel the presence of angels around you, leaving you in awe. Whether it's receiving a scholarship, marriage proposals, or being offered chocolate by a social influencer in a mall, gratitude is the key to opening the doors of miracles. Start loving the world around you; it will enhance your vibe. Journal about grateful behavior; jot down everything that comes to mind.

"If you don't like something, change it. If you can't change it, change your attitude." - Maya Angelou

Figure-7.1:Unlocking Miracle

Anything can happen; don't lose hope. When we are uncertain about our future, it is easier for us to stay positive because the future is not predefined. The law of uncertainty helps us become more positive. By believing that anything can happen, we gain the flexibility to change our thought processes and behaviors, allowing us to adapt our reactions.

The world is changing rapidly, and everything around us is advancing day by day. Technologies and innovations like computers, mobile phones, and artificial intelligence have taken over the world. This allows us to imagine the best-case scenarios because these advancements create various possibilities for good outcomes.

"Seeing, hearing, feeling, are miracles, and each part and tag of me is a miracle."-Walt Whitman

Life is unpredictable too along with time. No one could have imagined that the world would shut down during COVID-19, but it did. The world has suffered a lot, and there is much pain inside every human being. Embracing unpredictability can make you more confident, as your life could improve at any moment. It could even be tomorrow.

"A gentle word, a kind look, a good-natured smile can work wonders and accomplish miracles." - William Hazlitt

- **THE PLACEBO EFFECT:**

The placebo effect refers to the phenomenon wherein the power of the mind-body connection is harnessed to treat patients using substances devoid of therapeutic value, such as sugar pills or saline injections. Psychological therapies, alongside these inert treatments, have been shown to significantly enhance mental health. When patients receive only these placebo treatments, their belief in the efficacy of the intervention can lead to actual improvements in their health. This remarkable phenomenon, where the expectation of healing facilitates real physiological and psychological benefits, is known as the placebo effect.

SHIFT YOUR ENERGY:

Start writing your autobiography up to today. This will mentally help you generate a sense of achievement and provide inspiration for others. Next, begin reading biographies of famous scientists, personalities, and freedom fighters. After that, you can start envisioning your life in an ideal scenario. Understand that life may not unfold exactly according to this script, but eventually, you will find peace with yourself.

Work on your energies; cultivate feminine energy by embracing femininity and adjusting masculine traits if you're male.

Leave behind all the bad deeds; sinning usually blocks the good things coming into your life. For instance, imagine leaving home in the morning for work, and God has planned a breakthrough for you,a promotion or a billion-dollar deal, but just as you're about to leave, you argue with your mother or spouse over toast or tea that isn't to your liking. Congratulations, you may have missed your upcoming blessing over a cup of tea. God works in mysterious ways, so be kind and humble enough to protect your inner peace and the peace of others.

Search for uniqueness, patterns, and positivity; this is where miracles lie. A cool breeze on a hot summer day is a miracle for you.Forgive yourself and forgive others. The day you release all your baggage is the day you begin creating miracles in your life.Mend your relationships with family, parents, siblings, friends, teachers, and colleagues. You don't have to include them in your life; just clear your energy with them. Rainfall is the form of miracle,don't curse it.

- **FORGIVENESS:**

Let's forgive our biggest enemy, the one who has broken and shattered us into pieces. Forgiveness opens your heart to light, eventually changing your aura. Asking for forgiveness requires courage to accept your faults. Forgiveness is often considered a sign of weakness, but in reality, it is the highest virtue of life. It takes courage to admit wrongdoing and seek forgiveness. Not everyone understands the value of this virtue.

Forgiveness can erase all regrets; it is the path to repentance before God for our misdeeds. Over-apologizing can make you seem like a people-pleaser, while not accepting fault can portray you as egoistic. Balance your behavior; learn to apologize sincerely.Begin with your parents, starting with your mother, then your father, siblings, friends, and neighbors. Mend your relationship with God by acknowledging your sins and apologizing for any hurtful words you may have spoken.

Mend relationships with your spouse, children, or anyone you may have unintentionally hurt. Give them time to process and accept your apology; you've done your part. If you're unable to approach them directly due to shyness or fear of boosting their ego, visualize them with closed eyes and apologize. Repeat this practice often, and you'll see gradual changes in your life.

The second part of forgiveness requires great courage, to forgive others. When someone seeks forgiveness from you, forgive them. Forgive your archenemy, your heartbreaker, your parents for not valuing you, your spouse for not understanding you, your friends for not standing by you, and anyone who has not done justice to you. Forgive them for the sake of God. Release the burden from your life; keep your heart clean. Practice forgiveness every morning and every night before sleep.

Forgive them even if they aren't sorry or unwilling to admit their faults; they may be egoistic. Cleanse your soul and mind; ensure you do not allow them the freedom to hurt you again. Do not keep bringing them back into your life; always uphold your self-respect.

Forgive your deceased loved ones and ancestors; forgive them for any generational trauma they may have caused.

- **SUMMARY:**

1. Good things can happen anytime, anywhere; just expect them.
2. Miracles always happen with us, but we often don't pay attention to them.
3. Your soul could feel the miracle that is happening or about to happen.
4. Rain is the form of miracle,it takes a soul to recognise it.
5. Shift your energy by focusing on good.
6. Observe the uniqueness in nature.
7. Beauty is a miracle.
8. Unlock your upcoming miracles by forgiving others and asking forgiveness from others.
9. Good intentions open close doors.
10. Miracle happen when you feel connection with God.

CHAPTER EIGHT

THE BUTTERFLY EFFECT

"The fluttering of a butterfly's wings can effect climate changes on the other side of the planet." - Paul Erlich

Insignificant, tiny events can have a huge impact on a person's life. Your tiniest action can set off a domino effect. The flapping of butterfly wings is so powerful that it can cause a tornado. When you make a choice, this decision can lead you down a completely different path in life that you never imagined. Tiny habits like brushing your teeth at night, always greeting everyone first, or saying no to meetings you never wanted can trigger a chain reaction of inexplicable events or meaningful coincidences. These actions can align with your higher versions and help fulfill your dreams. Be grateful and deeply appreciate your current life. The tranquility in your heart will be priceless and divine.

Figure-8.1: Butterfly Effect

"The butterfly effect is a term used in chaos theory to describe how small changes to a seemingly unrelated thing or condition can affect large, complex systems." - Edward Lorenz (The meteorologist who coined the term "butterfly effect")

- **LAW OF ACCUMULATION:**

The Law of Accumulation states that very small or tiny efforts or habits can give us desired, effective results over time. Continuous efforts and gradual additions play a significant role in success. This process requires consistency and a lot of patience. For example, learning a language or playing a musical instrument demands regular practice and time. Practicing for 20 minutes daily can yield effective results within a year. Perseverance is essential to master this concept.

This principle is highly motivating because tiny efforts accumulate to produce significant outcomes. No matter how small the habit or saving, it can create substantial momentum. Small sacrifices can lead to great success. The accumulation of knowledge is crucial for research, and regular study helps achieve good grades and secure a bright future. However, consistency is a must in cultivating and understanding these tiny habits.

"Small shifts in your thinking, and small changes in your energy, can lead to massive alterations of your end result."-Kevin Michel

- **DOMINO EFFECT:**

The Domino Effect means that one small event can trigger a series of events in a cascading manner. This refers to a chain reaction where the first action leads to a sequence of subsequent actions. It can initiate a long chain of positive events, such as starting a donation drive and encouraging others to contribute to charity, which can result in significant successful outcomes. One small action can literally change the world around us and for others. Conversely, sometimes stepping back from an event can prevent a negative chain reaction that could cause harm.

The Domino Effect illustrates that when the first domino is triggered by a simple force, the subsequent dominoes fall on their own. This concept highlights how events can amplify through a sequence of reactions.

SUMMARY:

1. One tiny habit can literally change your overall personality.
2. Work on good things to create a positive chain reaction.
3. Tiny little things accumulate to form a bigger picture.
4. Your one word could cause a hurricane in somebody's life.

5. Your one good word or compliment could make someone's day.
6. Your one 'no' can stop an upcoming tsunami in your life.
7. Your one effort for charity can create a network of millions.
8. Your one post can raise awareness among millions.
9. Your one tiny habit can bring peace with a significant other.
10. Your one gift can resolve all your problems with another person.
11. One greeting can mend family issues from years ago.
12. One tiny change in habit can make you a billionaire.
13. One thought can shift your entire mindset.
14. One picture of you can make you viral and popular.
15. One reply to that person could result in your happily married life.
16. One job application could literally change your paradigm.
17. One activity can change your life.
18. Dedicate one day to saying yes to all things.
19. One day for deep-cleaning your room.
20. One day for a thorough body cleanse, like a spa day.

CHAPTER NINE

ALLOCATE 24 HOURS FOR SELF-CARE

"The future depends on what you do today."-Mahatma Gandhi

One day can help you change your miserable situation to a successful life. You can experience growth; you could decide to work on your personal development. Viral videos, hashtags, and trending posts could literally change your paradigm. You could shift from fearful situations to a strong mentality. Weather changes or natural disasters can alter the situation of an entire city. Global events and meetings could bring about significant changes. Financial conditions could gradually shift. There is always day one. One visit, one apology, one confession, one job offer, one idea, one disaster, one coincidence (part of a divine plan), one vote could literally change the government. One motivational speech. Give yourself one day with no complaints. Speak only the truth for one day. Try something new for one day."

"Everything happens for a reason and a purpose, and it serves you".- Anthony Robbins

Figure-9.1: Life Achieving Growth

• **FIND YOUR ULTIMATE GOAL OF LIFE:**

The ultimate goal in life may vary from person to person based on ethnicity and personal background. Goals may also change over time. However, what does any person truly want in life? While the desire for money is strong, and many people aim to earn more and more, ultimately, the goal should be to achieve peace and love.

Having a loving family and enjoying life's luxuries should be considered. Self-realization and inner harmony should be prioritized. Strive to build meaningful relationships, as mental peace is invaluable and cannot be bought. Greed and hatred have unfortunately permeated many areas of our hearts. A sound sleep, free of worries, should be a primary goal in life.

• DESTINATION ADDICTION:

Destination addiction is a psychological concept in which a person believes that happiness will be found in the future,be it the next job, relationship, task, or achievement. It is the belief that happiness will come only when a particular task is completed or a specific goal is achieved. Such individuals are always restless and never feel satisfied with their current situation, perceiving it as inadequate and always expecting unrealistic outcomes. Consequently, they remain anxious and are unable to fully enjoy life.

The societal pressure of achievement and success has caused many people to feel dissatisfied with their lives. Constant comparisons with others also contribute to this condition. Relationships often fail due to dissatisfaction with the present moment, and the urge to achieve something better and bigger fosters impatience.

"Make each day your masterpiece."-John Wooden

The solution to this problem lies in practices such as regular meditation, which helps one stay in the present moment. Avoiding unrealistic imaginings and starting a gratitude journal can also be beneficial. The key is to cultivate happiness with what you have right now.

"Don't count the days, make the days count."- Muhammad Ali

• VICTIM MINDSET:

The victim mindset is characterized by people blaming others for their misfortunes. They constantly seek sympathy from others, often feeling restless and angry, and may harbor a desire to retaliate against those who have wronged them. This trait can hinder self-improvement and personal growth, as well as affect professional development. Such a mindset may stem from past experiences or childhood trauma.

It is a psychological condition where a person perceives themselves as a victim of circumstances or others' actions. Recognizing this mindset through self-analysis is crucial. Once identified, take responsibility for your actions and seek help. The blame game will never lead to progress.

- **LAW OF SUBSTITUTION:**

The Law of Substitution means that when negative thoughts are replaced with positive ones, it can break the cycle of negative thinking. This shift leads to a positive mindset and can help you achieve emotional and mental maturity. By substituting negative thoughts with positive ones, you can overcome fears and anxiety.

- **CELEBRATE SMALL WINS:**

Celebration is also a practice of gratitude; involve only your well-wishers in celebrating your small wins. Share chocolates, as not everyone around you will be happy. Celebrate alone if needed. Visit your favorite place, talk to your favorite person, wear your favorite dress, find reasons to celebrate. This is another way to adopt a grateful attitude.

There is happiness in little things, like finding the right parking spot or discovering the perfect shade of nail polish. There's joy in the smooth glide of a pen on paper and the nostalgic scent that brings back good memories. Happiness lies in finding a perfect discount coupon or enjoying a well-made cup of tea or coffee. It's in stumbling upon a relatable meme or video, having a successful meeting without tough questions from your boss. Happiness is in writing a letter to a friend or expressing your feelings, enjoying a windy weather day, or gaining your boss's appreciation. There's joy in receiving a message or call from a favorite person or receiving flowers.

Celebrate these moments. Appreciation is also a form of celebration. Acknowledge all the happy moments with gratitude and happiness. Buy chocolates, bake cookies, gift flowers, or order food online. Prepare your favorite dish and express your gratitude to God for the people in your life. Be thankful for everything you've been given and avoid causing harm to others.

SUMMARY:

1. Give yourself 24 hours for self-love.
2. One day for deep work.
3. One day for deep cleaning.
4. One day for deep thoughts.
5. One day off from work.
6. One day for everything you enjoy.
7. One day to remove negative thoughts.
8. One day for the spa.
9. One day for your loved ones.
10. One day could literally change your whole life; make decisions wisely.
11. Give yourself 24 hours to break the pattern.
12. One day for sports.
13. One day for mental decluttering.
14. One day scheduled to call old friends.
15. One truth can change your entire life, creating a hurricane of events. Don't hide your emotions.

CHAPTER TEN

THE POWER OF TRUTH

"If you tell the truth, you don't have to remember anything" - Mark Twain

Be honest with yourself; honesty is true self-love. If you aim to live a healthy life, eliminate little lies from your life. As we discussed the butterfly effect in one's life, the ripple effect caused by dishonesty and being a liar could bring tornadoes into your life.

When you stop telling lies, you can literally increase your positive vibe and attract more blessings into your life. More blessings lead to more miracles, aligning you with your manifestations. Trust me, try not to tell lies for one week. It requires extreme courage to speak the truth about ourselves because it's easy to speak bitter truths about others, but being truthful about ourselves is painful.

"Honesty is the first chapter in the book of wisdom"- Thomas Jefferson

Figure-10.1: The Power of Truth

Take this as a sign: one decision, like speaking the truth, can cause a very positive butterfly effect in your life. The paradigm will shift, and eventually, everything will connect one day. That will mark the beginning of your new journey.Give yourself time to change; these effects are slow but extremely beneficial for maintaining good mental health.

'The truth will set you free."- Jesus Christ

- **THE POWER OF WORDS:**

It has been said that words have power. Words can make you or break you; speeches and stories can literally shape our society and culture. Political leaders like Mahatma Gandhi and Martin Luther King Jr. inspired many through their speeches about non-violence. Words can affect our mental state, and sometimes harsh criticism leads to poor performance. Even diplomacy can resolve many issues. Positive affirmations can impact our mental and physical health. When you feel good, you look good, and vice versa. Similarly, negative self-talk can affect our mood and turn our vibe more toxic. When you post a picture on social media, positive or negative comments from unknown people can change your entire mental state, even though the comments are not personal. Words can make or break you.

"The pen is mightier than the sword,"said Edward Bulwer-Lytton.

To attract more audiences and customers, advertisers use catchy slogans. Words are not just words; when you speak, you speak your mind. If your mind is a mess, your speech will reflect it. "Failure" is one of the most heartbreaking words. In my opinion, this word should be removed from academic report cards. When a child fails an exam, and teachers highlight the student's report card with the term "Failed," it can have a severe psychological impact on the student.

"Rather than love, than money, than fame, give me truth." - Henry David Thoreau

Control your tongue; speak good or remain silent. Your words can create positive or negative aura very quickly. Choose your words carefully when speaking to yourself or others.

When you look good, you feel good, and when you feel good, you treat others well. Be friendly but maintain your dignity by not being overly available. Respect yourself enough to walk away from situations and people who demoralize you.Track your mood according to dates; for females, moods change rapidly according to the four cycles.Do some inner work to understand what your heart yields, what it yearns for, and what it craves. It's okay to listen to your heart.

Be patient when things are going in the wrong direction, even after putting in all the efforts. Be patient when your feelings are hurt, when you are mentally abused, when you are openly betrayed, when you are cheated. Let karma do its work. Remain silent and patient, have faith in the Almighty. Sometimes, stand for justice when needed, and stand up for yourself and for those who are weaker.This attribute of life will eventually create a ripple effect.

Practice patience with family and friends. Understand their behavior, observe patterns; they might have psychological illnesses or hidden childhood traumas and insecurities. Track their habits and moods. Try to understand their hidden battles. But,once others get to know that you are patient, they may test your patience until you lose your cool. Decode their behavior and act accordingly. Ignore them as much as possible.

- **GRATITUDE IS A CHOICE:**

Choose to be grateful, even when you feel empty-handed. When you think you have nothing to be grateful for, you're at rock bottom in your life. Be grateful for your health, your hands, your brain, etc. If you are ill, be grateful for the good times you've had. Be grateful for the food you have. This is a choice; choose to count your blessings. Shift your mindset towards abundance. You never know what might unlock hidden blessings. When all doors seem closed, be grateful for the challenging times. That's when choosing gratitude matters most, because anyone can be grateful when they have everything.Find reasons to be grateful. Be thankful to the people around you who have supported you during tough times. Never take them for granted.

Let's take an example from video games. When we play a video game, we select an avatar with different features and skills. As we collect coins or points to unlock strengths and advance levels, our avatar becomes stronger and more capable. Similarly, in life, we are like avatars unlocking strengths and overcoming weaknesses by learning life's lessons. Gratitude enhances our blessings; this principle is found in the Holy Quran. Count your blessings every day, every night, or whenever you feel low or anxious.

Certainly, we may feel jealous or envious of others who seem to be at different stages in the game of life. One thing you can do to overcome this jealousy is to pray for them. Ask God to bless them more or protect their blessings. Set clear intentions; these good intentions may bring you more than what that person has, in unimaginable ways. This practice can open doors and attract blessings.

Choose gratitude and encourage others to appreciate what they already have, whether it's beauty, intelligence, emotional intelligence, kindness, wealth, or a helpful nature. Don't limit gratitude to material things. Choose friends who are grateful.

Gratitude brings serendipity, tranquility, and prosperity. It brings mental peace. When you start practicing gratitude, you will begin to notice coincidences, surprises, offers, gifts, and synchronicities.Don't be robotic; truly feel gratitude, raise your vibration, and cultivate a thought process by jotting down the good things in life. Embrace setbacks as opportunities for growth.

- **SUMMARY:**

1. Truth is the most powerful weapon to bring prosperity into your life.
2. Being truthful should not make you a harsh person.
3. Words have power; choose them wisely.
4. Being grateful for what you have is not a big deal. However, maintaining gratitude when you are at rock bottom makes you truly remarkable.
5. The words you choose are the real essence of your true personality.
6. Start practicing gratitude every day to bring more happiness and blessings.
7. Being truthful is a superpower.

8. Truth can change your vibe by shifting your vibrations.

Life Audit

A life audit is a practice to organize different sections of your life: personal, career, professional, friendships, relationships, self-love, physical health, mental health, spiritual life, and social networking. Firstly, analyze your life with honesty and without self-deception. Assess your level of satisfaction with your current situation. If you are not satisfied, identify the areas where improvement is needed and where you need to focus more to achieve greater success.Strive to find balance between your professional and personal life.

Take a diary and pen and answer these questions :

- Compare your current life with your dream life.
- Where do you see yourself in the coming years?
- How is your health right now?
- How can you improve your health? Is your health perfect?
- What is your BMI?
- What is your dream job?
- What is your current job?
- How do you rate your overall life out of 10?
- How is your confidence?
- Do you have peace in your life?
- Who hurts you the most?
- How are your friendships?
- How many close friends do you have?
- How is your relationship?
- Are you single? If yes, do you want to be in a relationship?
- What can you do to improve your life?
- What is stopping you from achieving your dream life?
- Do you need to distance yourself from certain people?
- Do you need to stop wasting time?
- What are you saving for in the future?
- How is your mental health?
- When did you last feel anxious?

- When was your last panic attack?
- How do you celebrate your birthdays?
- How would you like to celebrate your birthday?
- What are your hobbies?
- What are your strengths?
- What are your weaknesses?
- What are your interests?
- How do you entertain yourself?
- What is your dream car?
- What is your current financial situation?
- How do you practice self-love?
- What is your daily routine?
- How many hours of sleep do you get?
- What is your diet like?
- Which area of your life needs improvement?
- What is the biggest lesson you've learned in life?
- What is your most memorable moment?
- If you could bring someone back into your life, who would it be?

Make a routine to regularly check on your progress towards your goals. Learn new skills and work on improving your life. Stop worrying and start taking action.

Inner Work / Shadow Work

Answer these questions to get to know your inner self. Explore your hidden and suppressed emotions and fears:

- What are you hiding from others?
- What are you avoiding?
- What are you addicted to?
- Are you honest?
- What is your inner fear?
- Are you angry with yourself?
- Do you have any guilt?
- Are you desperate?
- What are you not letting go of?
- Were you traumatized in childhood?
- Do you lie to yourself?
- Do you prefer not to be around people?
- Have you ever felt betrayed?
- What is the hardest part of life for you?
- What do you want to change about your parents?
- Do you forgive easily?
- What is love in your terms?
- Where could you find peace?
- Have you ever felt appreciated?
- Are you jealous of someone?
- Have you been bullied?
- When was the last time you cried?
- When was the last time you laughed so much?
- When did you feel loved?
- Have you experienced love at first sight?
- What advice would you give to your childhood self?
- Have you ever faced trauma?
- Do you feel comfortable at home?
- Are you avoiding your spouse?

- Have you ever felt like you're not good enough?
- When you look in the mirror, what do you feel?
- Do you see your face when you close your eyes?
- Are you truly happy or pretending to be?
- Are you in love with someone?
- Do you have a crush?
- Have you confessed your love to someone?
- Are you running from something?
- Is there a void within you?
- Have you ever felt nauseous or had a panic attack?
- What does your inner child need right now?
- What would you say to yourself when you meet your 10-year-old self?
- Have you ever felt like ending your life?
- Do you have an ego issue?
- Do you have attachment issues?
- Has anyone in your family needed a psychiatrist?
- Whom do you want to prove something to?
- Do you work to avoid your feelings?
- Are you afraid to open up your feelings?

Start Journalling

Consider various aspects of your life:

- Health: Evaluate your physical and mental health.
- Career: How is your career progressing? Are you at peace with your professional life?
- Finances: What is your financial situation? What steps are needed to improve it?
- Entertainment: Do you have time for fun and relaxation?
- Family and Relationships: Are you spending quality time with your family? How is your love life?
- Current Status vs. Future Goals: What is your current status, and what do you want it to be in the future?
- Resilience: How do you handle the ups and downs of life?
- Spirituality: Are you spiritually active, or do you need to work on your connection with a God?
- Identify where you are currently and where you want to be,this is your destination.

Letter Activity

- Write a letter to your past version?
- Write a letter to your future version?
- Write a love letter to yourself?
- Write letter to your loved ones?
- Write an appreciation letter to your boss or colleague?
- Write a letter to God?

About The Author

Farha Khan, the author of this book, serves as an assistant professor at an esteemed engineering college. She holds a Master's degree in Digital Communication, showcasing her expertise in the field. Driven by her fervent passion for writing, blogging, and journaling, she transformed her aspirations of becoming an author into a tangible reality. Her unwavering belief in the adage "Good intentions open the blocked doors" reflects her optimistic outlook on life.

Contact detail: Farhakhan1609@gmail.com